CAPE CANAVER
PHOTOGRAPI
BY
CHUCK ROGERS

Dedicated to Bob Special
and to my fellow workers:
Ashley Abel, Marty Barron, Cal Bennett, Juan Billingsley, Alex Bosmeny, Al Bransford,
Bob Breland, Ray Buchanan, Ben Bundy, Arny Cain, Christine Caldwell, Ernie Caldwell,
Jeff Carlin, Ron Carmen, Bill Carter, Fay Caughron, Minus Cessac, John Chambers,
Jim Clevenger, Barney Corbin, Lane Couey, Richard Crowe, Bob Day, Bill Deac, Don DeFillips,
George Dill, Irv Doty, Paul Douglas, John Esposito, Bill Evans, Jim Farley, Gene Ferguson,
Joe Ficarrotta, Bob Figlioli, John Fleming, Rosey Flowers, Bill Ford, Bill French, Max Fundom,
Les Gaver, Bill Gibson, Joe Giles, Steve Gilley, Tom Glende, Fred Graham, Brandy Griffith,
Walt Haessner, Bob Hamelin, Olie Hansen, Bruce Hoover, Russ Hopkins, John Hunter,
Otis Imboden, Bill Irwin, Bud Janes, Len Johnson, Glen Jones, Clay Kelty, Joel Kirkland, Dick Kise,
Dave Kovljain, Walt Langston, Karl LaRoche, Bill Larson, Tom Mahle, Luis Marden,
Mac McClellan, Jim McNearny, George Meguire, Bill Moore, Tom Moran, Tom Nebbia,
Pappy Neener, George Neven, Joe Nores, Bill Olson, Yvonne Patrick, Baldy Peele,
John Perryman, J.W. Peterson, Hugh Pinney, Jack Piszczek, Joe Przyborski, Pete Quadagno,
Art Reed, Jack Richards, Dick Roberts, Emile Rochefort, Lenord Rochefort, Lou Roquevert,
Fred Santomassino, Ralph Schorer, Richard Schultz, Ken Senstad, Bill Seward, Pat Shea, Cecil Staughton,
Jim Sullivan, Larry Summers, Bill Taub, Ed Thomas, Tyler Tinker, Merv Tyrrell, Ed VanBuren,
Erv Walker, Frank Wally, Bob Walrath, Bill Weimer, Wes Westberg, Frank Westbrook, Bill Wiest,
Klaus Wilkens, Marion Wilkerson, Red Williams, Charlie Wilson, Dick Winer, Tom Wyman.
Also to my friends:
Howard Benedict, Ken Grine, Art Lord, Russ Yoder and Dick Young

Chuck Rogers photographing an Atlas missile with a
Deardorff 8x10 view camera. Photo: Jim McNearny

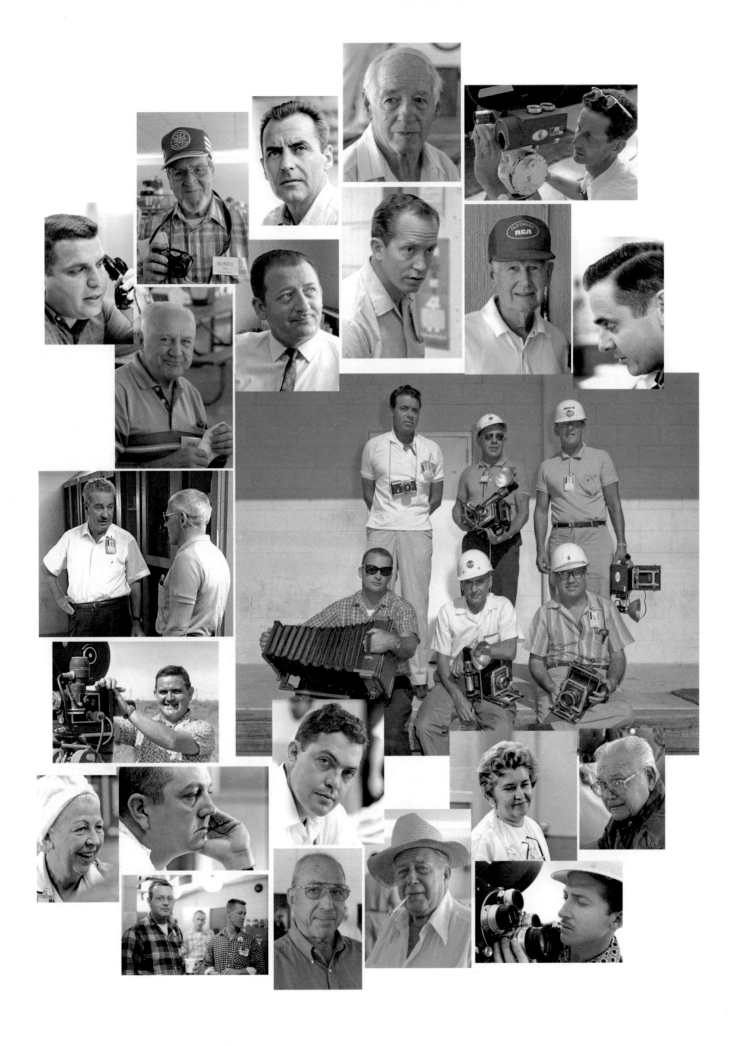

Bob Special and John Morrison

1958 Vanguard 3

1958 Vanguard 3

1958 Bomarc - The seagull was so surprised that it stopped in mid-air. Life magazine used it full page inside the back cover.

1958 Douglas Thor-Able Lunar Probe

1958 Atlas 6B

1958 Navaho

1958 Jupiter

1957 ABMA Jupiter

1960 Atlas Able V

1959 Juno II with 50 foot towers used by photographers

NO SMOKING WITHIN 100 FT.

QUID OXYG

1959 Juno II

1958 ABMA Juno II Lunar Probe

1960 July 20
First Polaris launch
from submerged sub

First three-page
fold-out ever published
in the
National Geographic

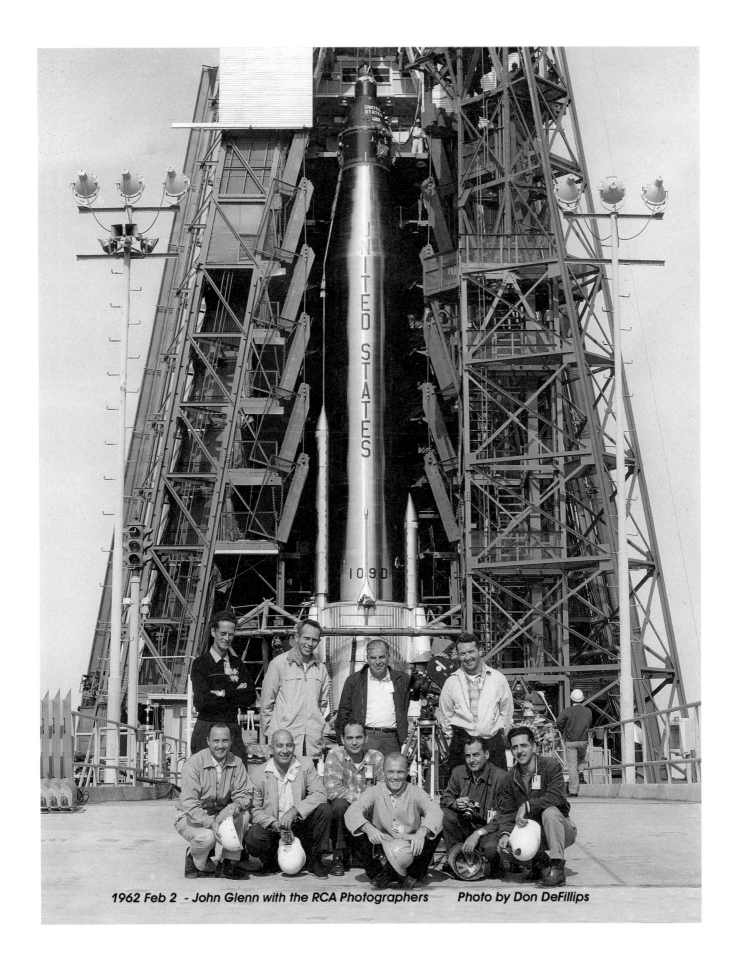

1962 Feb 2 - John Glenn with the RCA Photographers   Photo by Don DeFillips

1962 Feb 22 - President Johnson welcomes John Glenn back from orbit.

President John F. Kennedy
Photographed by Chuck Rogers at Cape Canaveral seven days before his death.
Shown with Senator George Smathers. Copyright Chuck Rogers

Alan Sheppard

1961 Sheppard Launch

1966 Saturn 5 - First Roll-out

1981 Shuttle pre-launch

SINGER supplied electronics for the Shuttle.
I was hired by them to go from Atlanta to the
Kennedy Space Center and return with a photo
suitable for a two-page spread in the SINGER ANNUAL REPORT.
This accomplished that assignment.

Made in the USA
Columbia, SC
08 November 2024